ADVENTURES IN CULTURE

HOMES AROUND THE WORLD

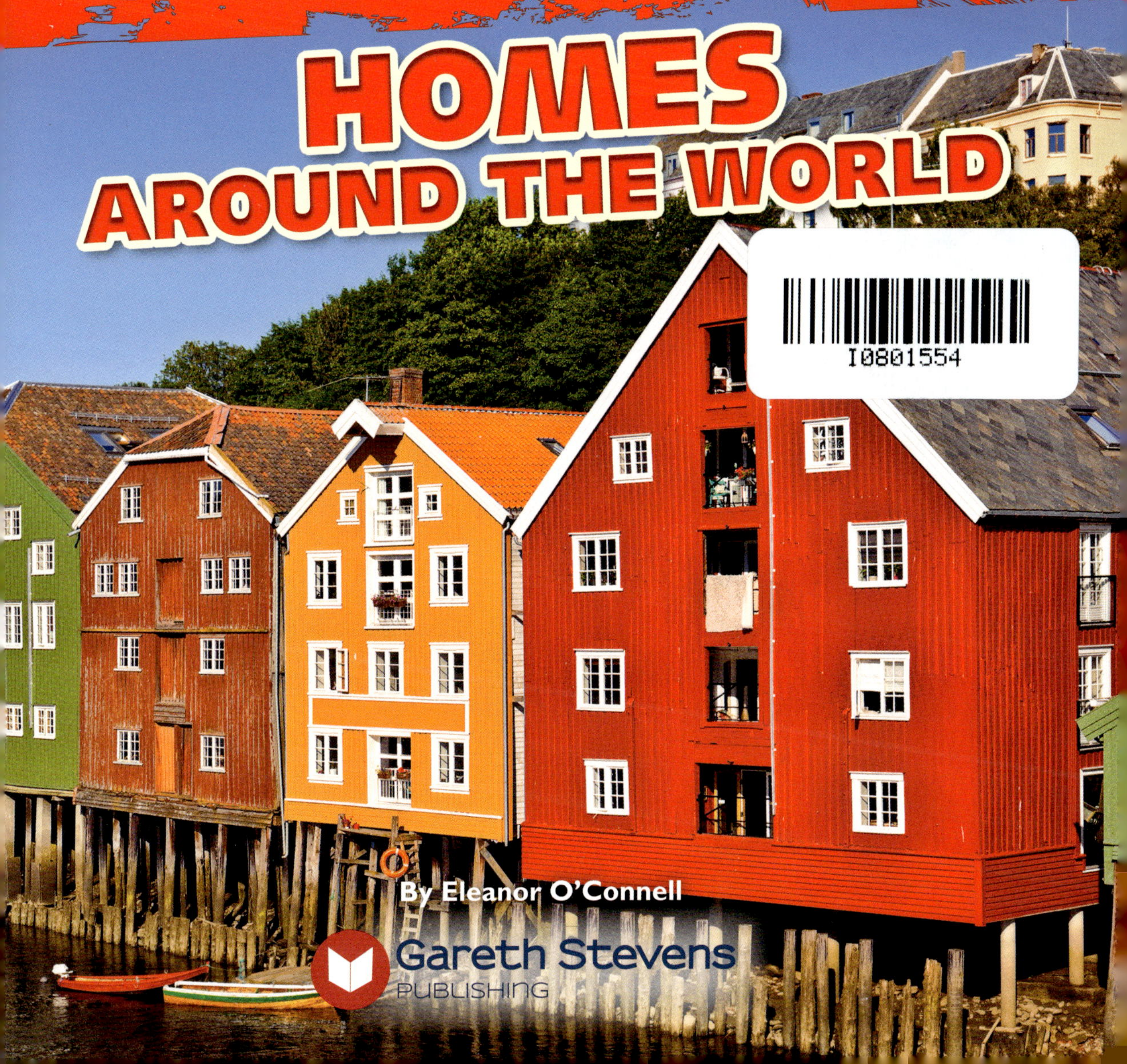

By Eleanor O'Connell

Gareth Stevens PUBLISHING

Please visit our website, www.garethstevens.com. For a free color catalog of all our high-quality books, call toll free 1-800-542-2595 or fax 1-877-542-2596.

Cataloging-in-Publication Data

Names: O'Connell, Eleanor.
Title: Homes around the world / Eleanor O'Connell.
Description: New York : Gareth Stevens Publishing, 2017. | Series: Adventures in culture | Includes index.
Identifiers: ISBN 9781482455861 (pbk.) | ISBN 9781482458817 (library bound) | ISBN 9781482455878 (6 pack)
Subjects: LCSH: Dwellings–Juvenile literature. | Dwellings–Cross-cultural studies–Juvenile literature.
Classification: LCC GT172.O54 2017 | DDC 643'.1–dc23

Published in 2017 by
Gareth Stevens Publishing
111 East 14th Street, Suite 349
New York, NY 10003

Designer: Andrea Davison-Bartolotta and Bethany Perl
Editor: Therese Shea

Photo credits: Cover, p. 1 Tatiana Popova/Shutterstock.com; pp. 2–24 (background texture) Flas100/Shutterstock.com; p. 5 (house) TTphoto/Shutterstock.com; p. 5 (apartment) Ryan DeBerardinis/Shutterstock.com; p. 7 romana chapman/Getty Images; p. 9 photography by baoshabaotian/Getty Images; p. 11 Richard Majlinder/Getty Images; p. 13 Radiokafka/Shutterstock.com; p. 15 ERIC LAFFORGUE/Getty Images; p. 17 javarman/Shutterstock.com; p. 19 George Steinmetz/Getty Images; p. 21 pikselstock/Shutterstock.com.

Printed in the United States of America

CPSIA compliance information: Batch #CW17GS: For further information contact Gareth Stevens, New York, New York at 1-800-542-2595.

CONTENTS

Welcome Home! 4
Tree Houses. 6
Farmers' Caves 8
Queenslanders 10
Yurts. 12
Tata Somba Houses 14
Tongkonan 16
Floating Homes 18
Reed Houses 20
Glossary. 22
For More Information. 23
Index 24

Boldface words appear in the glossary.

Welcome Home!

What is a home? Most would say it's a place to rest and eat. Homes can look different, from apartments in a city to houses in the country. In this book, you'll see homes from around the world. Think about which you'd like to live in!

country house
city apartment

Tree Houses

You might have a backyard tree house. Some people in Southeast Asia live in tree houses! Floods can't harm homes high in trees. Tree houses also can't be **trampled** by large animals, such as elephants.

Farmers' Caves

In China, more than 30 million people live in *yaodongs* (yow-DOHNZ), also called farmers' caves. People dig these caves into mountainsides or into the sides of a giant hole in the ground. Caves are cool in summer and warm in winter.

Queenslanders

Queenslanders are a kind of home in Australia. They're raised off the ground. This lets air flow under the house and keep it cool. Queenslanders also have a covered **porch** called a veranda that allows people to stay outside while it's raining.

veranda

Yurts

A yurt (or *ger*) is a round, movable, tent-like home often found in Mongolia in central Asia. Mongolians sometimes need to travel with herds of animals. They can easily take down their yurt and move it to a new place.

Tata Somba Houses

Found in west Africa, *Tata Somba* houses—made of wood, mud, and straw—have two floors. The first floor is for keeping animals and cooking. The second floor is for sleeping and is open to the sky. **Towers** with straw roofs hold dried grain.

tower

Tongkonan

Tongkonan are the special homes of the Torajan people of Indonesia. A *tongkonan* roof is curved like a boat. There are often wooden **carvings** of plants and animals in its walls, too. According to **myths**, the first *tongkonan* was made in heaven!

Floating Homes

Many people in the Netherlands live below sea level. That means when it rains, floods may harm their houses. People have built houses on **stilts**. They've also built houses that rise with floodwaters and even float on the water!

Reed Houses

On Lake Titicaca in South America, native people live on islands made of **reeds** and plants that grow in the water. These people, the Uros, make reed homes, too. All over the world, people use **natural resources** to make special homes!

GLOSSARY

carving: a shape or figure made by cutting

myth: a story that was told by a people to explain a practice, belief, or natural event

natural resource: something that is found in nature and is useful to humans

porch: a part of a building attached to the entrance that has a roof and that may or may not have walls

reed: a tall, thin grass that grows in wet areas

stilt: one of a set of posts that are used to hold a building above water or the ground

tower: a tall, narrow building that may stand apart from or be connected to another building

trample: to cause harm by walking or stepping on something

FOR MORE INFORMATION

BOOKS

Laroche, Giles. *If You Lived Here: Houses of the World.* Boston, MA: Houghton Mifflin Books for Children, 2011.

Lewis, Clare. *Homes Around the World.* Chicago, IL: Heinemann Library, 2015.

Moore, Max. *Homes Around the World.* New York, NY: DK, 2009.

WEBSITES

Explore Japan: Housing, Food, and Clothes
web-japan.org/kidsweb/explore/housing/
Read about homes and other topics in Japan.

Kids Around the World
www.factmonster.com/ipka/A0930058.html
Find out more about how kids around the world live.

INDEX

Australia 10

China 8

farmers' caves 8

houses on stilts 18

Indonesia 16

Lake Titicaca 20

Mongolia 12

Netherlands, the 18

Queenslanders 10

reed homes 20

South America 20

Southeast Asia 6

Tata Somba houses 14

tongkonan 16

Torajan people 16

tree houses 6

Uros people 20

west Africa 14

yaodongs 8

yurt 12